Think Like A Greek Philosopher

Improve Your Critical Thinking,
Persuasion Skills,
and Style of Inquiry with Socratic
Questioning

Written by
Steven Schuster

rendering medical, legal or other professional advice or services. If professional assistance is required, the services of a competent professional person should be sought. The author shall not be liable for damages arising herefrom. The fact that an individual, organization of website is referred to in this work as a citation and/or potential source of further information does not mean that the author endorses the information the individual, organization to website may provide or recommendations they/it may make. Further, readers should be aware that Internet websites listed in this work might have changed or disappeared between when this work was written and when it is read.

For general information on the products and services or to obtain technical support, please contact the author.

Table of Contents

Introduction

Hi, my name is Socrates and my thoughts changed the world. But that's a very bold and conceited statement for an introduction so allow me to tell you my story. As I write this book now, I'm sitting in a jail cell at the outskirts of Athens. Within minutes, a guard is going to bring me a drink. It will be a cup of hem lock, which is poisonous. I shall empty the cup following which act I will become very sleepy and shut my eyes forever soon afterward. But before that happens, I wanted to share some of my ideas with you.

I was born in Athens in ancient Greece. I was always a private person and I'd like to keep this habit in my last moments, too. Without too many personal details, I'm comfortable to confess that I have the reputation of a mysterious troublemaker in my homeland. People refer to me as the first Western philosopher but I don't indulge in such self-polishing thoughts. Philosophers usually flatter themselves thinking they know a lot about the world. I really don't think I know that much at all.

The Peloponnesian war left a mark on my mind and after returning to Athens, I isolated myself to think a bit. In my time wisdom was the coolest label you could possess. If someone gathered a large support group behind his ideas, he was proclaimed wise. I took such "wisdom" with a large grain of salt. I my experience a lot of people who seem to be or claim to be wise are not actually that wise. This naturally proposes a problem. Those who believe in the authority of this sage, will blindly follow him, often at the cost of severe consequences.

Questioning wisdom helps you discover flaws in it. If you don't question, knowledge stands still as a rock instead of flowing and carving new ground like a river. Following this realization I started asking questions more intentionally.

I discovered that questioning a claim of something being true, tests its validity. If you question someone and they can prove that their claim is legit, great job. You made sure you're not signing up for spreading false information and you also helped someone practice to defend their truth.

For example, if someone claims that it is essential to worship the god Ares, I would ask, "What is essentialism? What is worshipping? Are there other gods to worship?" If they can't articulate what essentialism is, how can they claim that it is essential to worship Ares? If they can't explain what worship is, how can they know if they are really worshipping Ares, and therefore that they are doing an essential act?

If someone making claims can't answer the challenges imposed by questioning, then how can they state that their claim is true?

Plato, a very bright young man used to follow me around Athens, learning my questioning style which he would eventually bestow upon his student – Aristotle. He became the teacher of Alexander the Great. Alexander spread these teachings in his large kingdom. Eventually, the Romans occupying Alexander's empire helped spread this questioning tradition even further. After the Roman Empire fell apart, this precious knowledge rested idle for centuries until the miracle of the Renaissance happened. People started reading again the works of Plato and Aristotle and re-discovered the power of methodical questioning, and testing of claims –

the style you today know as Socratic Questioning.
I feel honored by the label.

Questioning gets a bad reputation. Some
mistakenly think that asking a question or many
questions, means that the question maker is
uneducated, or unwise. I think the opposite.

True wisdom lies in the knowledge of
acknowledging how little we actually know.

When one gets to this realization, they can start
asking questions and get to more accurate facts.
This being said, I must warn you that asking
questions can also be a quick way to make people
resentful.

I'm guilty of embarrassing a handful of very
important men in Athens who took my questions
very personally. If my questions highlighted their
ignorance, they took it even worse. When these
important people saw that others started to ask

question like I did, I was arrested for corrupting the fine people of Athens. Plato wrote a noteworthy piece about my trial and how I fought to defend myself utilizing the same questioning style I was arrested for. Needless to say that this made my enemies even more bitter.

I was convicted. The court made the mistake of asking me what I believed my punishment should be. I answered that they should feed me with a tasty meal every night at the sacred heart of the city to honor my achievement of opening up the eyes of the people of Athens to real wisdom. My enemies did not appreciate neither my wit nor my suggestion, they assessed that my insolence is beyond redemption so they sentenced me to death.

I haven't got much time left so I'll leave you with this: remember, the only thing you know for certain is that you know nothing. But don't take my word for it for I know nothing as well.

Chapter 1. Who Was Socrates?

Socrates was a man shrouded in mystery. He bucked the typical Athenian standards of his time (c. 470-399 BCE), and yet what little we do know about him comes from secondhand sources with questionable reliability.[1]

Surprisingly, for one of the world's most well-known philosophers, Socrates wrote nothing himself, but over the passing centuries has almost become a character with differing personality traits depending on the era the author is writing in or traits the author believes to be important.[1]

Much of what has been written about Socrates has been rejected as false and referring back to historical sources rather than more modern versions, which have taken certain liberties, tells us that Socrates stood out even among his contemporaries in Athens. In an age where good looks and maintaining a healthy body were viewed as directly tied to success, the historical sources all readily agree that Socrates was horribly unattractive in every way, including looking as if he'd skipped a significant number of meals rather than having the preferred aesthetic of a "potbelly."[1] In fact, historical accounts as well as drawings and busts from this period look nothing like the later statues depicting Socrates with a more handsome visage.[1] These more attractive images are what is most commonly used on websites and dust jackets today.[1]

Beyond being recognizable for his notoriously bad appearance, Socrates was also a well-known and controversial person in Athens to the point he was often mocked in plays by other philosophers of the era.[2] When Socrates was alive, he was often in plays as the butt of jokes, and he was often the subject of much comic ridicule. Aristophanes' *The Clouds* is a perfect example of this.[2] In his play, Aristophanes uses Socrates as the main character to show the immorality and atheism immediately following the deeper examination of language and nature, none of which is an accurate portrayal of philosophical study.[2]

However, it is also important to acknowledge that Socrates had his supporters as well, but much of their work wasn't performed until after his death. For example, Plato's *Apology of Socrates* is allegedly the defense given by Socrates at his trial when he was charged for irreverence toward the gods of Athens.[1] In this "apology," Plato depicts Socrates as a man who has integrity, intellect, control of himself and his emotions, and also someone who possessed exceptional skills to frame an argument for discussion or debate.[2] It's important to note that despite their significant age difference—Plato was an infant when *The Clouds* was produced circa 423 BCE—the relationship between Plato and Socrates was that of a mentor/mentee.[2]

In addition, we are also provided insight into Socrates' personality by Aristotle. In 367 BCE, Aristotle attended Academy, a school owned by Plato.[2] Because we know Socrates and Plato had such a close relationship, it is highly unlikely Socrates' methods and ideas would not have been discussed in the school. In later writings about Socrates, Aristotle says that Socrates asked questions, but he declined to give answers, and that was because he lacked the knowledge to be able to do so.[2] Aristotle further said Socrates looked to define the virtues, but that he did not spend his time studying nature, but rather ethics.[2]

In the years leading up to Socrates' trial and subsequent death, it is important to note that due to the Peloponnesian War, the military force had been fighting against Sparta for thirty years, and this had granted Athenian citizens a significant amount of freedom provided they didn't disrupt the democracy or break the law.[2] However, in 399 BCE, Socrates was charged with irreverence toward the gods. In the years during and immediately following the Peloponnesian War, there were several attempts to overthrow the democracy of Athens as well as several religious scandals that had primed both the public and officials. There was a definite expectation after the previous events that future perpetrators would be brought up on charges.[2]

The mood of the Athenians was further soured as they particularly did not like Socrates. This is clearly expressed in Plato's *Apology of Socrates*.[2] In *Apology* we see Socrates as someone who has tried over and over again to do his best by his community, but no matter what he does, they are looking for a martyr to sacrifice.

Socrates, who is not a wealthy man, also has no political influence and knows he will be found guilty and face death despite his desire and genuine attempts to help the people of Athens.[2] In the end, Socrates was found guilty of impiety and he was sentenced to death for his crimes.[1]

The death of Socrates is almost as famous as Socrates is as a philosopher in modern culture. Most people can immediately tell you how Socrates died—he committed suicide by drinking a cup of poison hemlock. To be clear, Socrates did this because that is how Athenians carried out death sentences at the time, and Socrates was made to become his own executioner. Socrates had earnestly tried to win his trial, but his attitude and previous history worked against him. As a philosopher, we also find ourselves relying significantly on others and their impressions of Socrates in order to form our own assessment of Socrates' own ideas, thoughts, and assessments. This makes Socrates and the techniques he used as a philosopher something of a mystery, but this book will introduce you to those techniques and teach you to use them so you can feel comfortable using them in your everyday life. The goal of this book is to teach you Socratic questioning to help you engage in this disciplined type of questioning to assist you in reaching your goals, no matter what they may be.

On Virtue

In the previous section, it's discussed that Aristotle, a student of Plato, gleaned quite a significant amount of information about Socrates due to Plato's relationship with Socrates and that we can reason it to be a fairly accurate assessment of Socrates' actions, abilities, and analysis of big life questions, i.e., what is virtue? What is justice? Unlike other philosophers, Socrates emphatically claimed that he never taught, and his personal style of philosophizing was through conversation.[2]

Because such a significant amount of Socrates' work as a philosopher was done in this unique way, there are virtually no published works by Socrates we can look at and analyze in order to learn more about his methods for Socratic questioning. However, one of Plato's contemporary philosophers and a follower of Socrates, Xenophon, compiled many of Socrates' conversations and exchanges in his book *Memorabilia*.

In Xenophon's book, we can see a pattern of topics Socrates would hold conversations about repeatedly. He was even accused at one point of continuing to discuss the same topics from years prior. Socrates' witty comeback focuses on the consistency of his performance as he has not only continued to discuss the same topics, but he's also continued to say the same things about the topics, not wavering in his stance a single time.

Socrates also brings up such topics as encouraging individuals to care for their soul and to make it as wonderful as possible. This is an interesting topic considering Socrates' own viewpoint of atheism and his subsequent charges for impiety and sentence to death when found guilty for such charges. Socrates also discusses his thoughts that depraved actions are committed due to a lack of knowledge, and his firm belief that it is better to be the victim of an injustice rather than commit an injustice. Many of Socrates' conversations are well known to discuss how a person "should" live or "ought" to live. This is one of the most common repeating themes in Socrates' list of topics. Socrates likes to focus on the ethics of life more than any other area of philosophy.

Spending time in deep thought considering how one "ought" to live is not a common pastime for the majority of people. Most people live their lives by a set of standards or norms they grew up with and exist as part of their cultural or societal norms. In Socrates' opinion, individuals do need to question and challenge these norms rather than follow them blindly. Taking the time to seriously question how one lives and deeply thinking about the answer has the potential to have a profound effect on our lives. This practice can be done day by day, allowing individuals to make positive choices as their lives change.

Practicing this type of analysis can be life changing, but it requires self-knowledge. The individual has to be able to look inward and truly analyze their nature and the values that shape their life. Socrates himself said, "The unexamined life is not worth living."[3] Assessing oneself and taking stock of who you are is one of the best decisions you can make. By engaging in this practice, you will learn, at a minimum, how you should live your life. Once you have that information, you have the ability to consciously make decisions on how to best care for yourself.

Socrates famously said, "Our true self is our soul." Because Socrates lived before the Christian Era, it's difficult to know exactly what he means by the term soul, but there is a clear understanding the term lacks the significance tied to the religious aspect currently used to define the term. According to Socrates, "It is the state of our soul or inner being, which determines our quality of life."[4] However, in contradiction to this, the vast majority of people believe they can identify what type of things are heavenly and what type of things are evil.[5] Generally, wealth, social acceptance, power, and status are all seen as universally good and signs of success. Consequently, poverty, social rejection, pain, and death are all considered to be outward signs of evil. It stands to reason that over the course of time this will be proven to be untrue. However, having a false idea of what makes a person happy can lead to a person indiscriminately chasing that thing in an attempt to be "happy" or to achieve inner peace, but once that thing has been attained, the person realizes attaining an item or status was not the goal, self-knowledge was the goal.

In Socrates' mind, the greatest good possible was virtue, which is demonstrated when a person shows moral excellence. A virtuous person is someone who actively engages in virtuous behavior while also maintaining positive moral character. Virtuous behaviors can include such behaviors as kindness, honesty, service, and gratitude. These are just some of the behaviors, as there are plenty more a person can choose to consciously practice these behaviors.[6]

Discussions on the topic of virtues was also a common occurrence for Socrates. He believed that when a person correctly defined virtue, they would naturally have to see its true value as the greatest good, which would lead them to happiness as they performed the "good" task. This happiness would then lead the person to automatically behaving in a virtuous manner.

Essentially, Socrates' thoughts can be expressed like so: Knowledge = Virtue = Happiness.

One of the key problems with Socrates' theory is that if happiness is so easy to attain, why do so many people choose not to become virtuous and prefer to engage in evil acts? In Socrates' mind, the answer is because a lot of people are ignorant. To Socrates, individuals engaging in evil acts don't realize what they're doing is evil, because if they did, they wouldn't choose to engage in those behaviors. Because Socrates considers these evil acts to be committed out of ignorance, they are done involuntarily, giving the individual no free will to make a decision either way.

In Plato's writing we see Socrates stating that individuals who commit evil acts fail to realize that behaving in a virtuous manner is the greatest possible good and that being virtuous will bring them happiness. Instead, Socrates believes people fall into the trap of committing evil acts because they falsely believe privileges like wealth, power, and pleasure are the best possible goods that exist, and evil acts are committed in an attempt to gain those privileges. In Socrates' worldview, the person who engages in evil acts doesn't realize he's besmirching his own soul and putting himself on a path to perpetual misery. The cluelessness of not being able to recognize what will make a person happy starts this cycle of bad behavior that repeats itself as the person thinks they know what will make them happy, but never experiences that fulfillment.

Interestingly, this is a concept many criminals have brought into the modern era as they've tried to justify their crimes to themselves and to others. It has also been used as a way to mitigate guilt so the perpetrator can feel better about their involvement in the crime or simply tell themselves whatever they need to hear to make having committed the criminal act something they can live with.[7] The most common themes used to justify a criminal's illegal actions include:

Denial of responsibility" is when an offender proposes that he or she was forced by the circumstances they were in to commit a crime; "denial of injury" means insisting that the crime was harmless; "denial of the victim" involves the belief that the person on the receiving end was asking for it; and "condemnation of the condemners" is when the criminal claims that those criticizing or dishing out punishment are doing so out of spite or to shift the blame from themselves. The final method, "appealing to higher loyalties," involves the perpetrator believing that the law needs to be broken for the good of a smaller section of society—for example, a gang or a group of friends.[8]

In addition to providing justification for crimes, we've also learned through the study of the brain that the criminal mind isn't really all that different from the non-criminal mind. Think back to any news broadcast you may have seen recently about serial killers. Joseph James DeAngelo, the Golden State Killer, was recently identified through a controversial familial DNA match after one of his relatives voluntarily submitted DNA to a commercial genomics company. From the outside looking in, Joseph DeAngelo seemed perfectly normal. He was married in 1973 and had three daughters. However, during that time, DeAngelo also committed thirteen murders and more than fifty rapes, earning him the name, the Golden State Killer.

When people think about the monster who committed the horrible and disturbing crimes, there is a strong idea that this person must set themselves apart in some way, but more often than not, what we see is the ability to hide in plain sight. This was not a skill unique to Joseph DeAngelo. Other serial killers were known to have this same ability and to be able to charm their way out of difficult situations. Ted Bundy worked at a crisis hotline for people contemplating suicide with the now-famous true crime author Anne Rule. Doctor Harold Shipman had a clinical practice comprised mostly of elderly women, where he injected them with large doses of painkillers in order to murder them so he could gain access to their money. In these cases, and many more, the perpetrator committing the evil act seemed perfectly normal, your average everyday citizen. In some cases, the individuals posed as someone who had been injured or needed assistance in order to gain their victim's trust and sympathy. We know from these cases and many more just like them that appearances can't be taken for granted as a true marker of identity and personality.

How to Get to Know Your Soul

Before you learn the ins and outs of Socratic questioning, it's important that you take Socrates' advice and discover who you truly are on the inside. In this process, it will be important for you to examine your inner world as well as your values. This will be the start of a lifelong journey of self-discovery. Just don't anticipate having life all figured out. That type of thinking and trying to answer life's big questions takes a lot of self-discovery and discipline.

Taking the time to get to know yourself is the ongoing process of understanding who you—the human being—really are on a level that is much deeper than the surface. The goal is to get at what really motivates you and how you view your inner world. Depending on what you see, this may also mean taking the plunge and really examining your insecurities, your self-doubt, and anything else that prevents you from putting your life under a microscope for a full and thorough examination.[9]

It's important to acknowledge right from the start that this is not an easy task, and it's one that takes dedication and commitment, but the rewards gleaned from self-examination and knowing your values and what you want to achieve in life are worth the hard work you'll put in. Once you know what is truly important to you, you'll be able to live by those values and beliefs and ensure others respect them. Knowing yourself this intimately allows you to prioritize things based on who you are. You'll have a different respect for your body and treat it with the kindness it deserves.[9]

There are numerous benefits to really knowing yourself. You'll know where you excel in life and where you could use some additional work to reach your goals. Knowing who you are means you'll know all about your personality quirks and that you won't let them stop you from discovering your life's purpose.[9]

The idea that you've grown up and subsequently aged with yourself and therefore must truly know yourself on the most fundamental levels is a false narrative. In this scenario there hasn't been the intent and purpose required to take on such a complicated endeavor as learning about your true self. You likely haven't asked yourself any of life's most complicated questions: Why do I exist? What is my purpose in life? What are my values and how do they shape my life? These types of questions take time to think about and work through because it's also very important that you don't simply mimic cultural and societal norms passed down to you by your parents or through heritage. You have the opportunity here to decide what is important to you and create your own set of values to live by.

So getting to know yourself… how do you do that exactly? That's a great question, because there are five categories of things you need to know about yourself that will help you become successful. Once these categories are listed, there will be questions in each category designed to help the reader reach the goal of looking inward and learning more about who they are.[10]

1. **Get to know your personality**

    To your best knowledge, how do other people perceive you?

    How confident are you in your ability to make decisions for yourself?

    What brings you joy?

    What gifts do you bring?

    Why does the world need the gifts you bring?

    Who needs the gifts you bring?

    What verb best describes you?

    When do you feel the most like yourself?

What makes you feel great about yourself?

What kinds of conversations do you have with your closest friends?

2. Get to know your core values

What is your highest core value?

What is your biggest self-limiting belief?

Who is the most important person in your life?

What is something that is true for you no matter what?

What is your moral compass in making difficult decisions?

What gives your life meaning?

What's missing from your life? From the world?

What do other people always thank you for?

What are you willing to struggle for?

3. Get to know your body

How comfortable are you with your own mortality?

What's memorable about you?

What makes you lose track of time?

4. Get to know your dreams

What kind of legacy do you want to leave behind?

What is one failure that you have turned into your greatest lesson?

How is life calling you?

If money wasn't an issue, what would you do with your time?

What kind of person do you want to be in five years?

What did you imagine you'd be doing right now when you were fifteen years old?

Who inspires you most? What qualities do they possess that inspire you?

5. Get to know your likes and dislikes

How would you like others to perceive you?

How do you want to make others feel?

If you had to teach something, what would you teach?

What makes you smile?

What are you drawn to?[10]

Chapter 2: How to Implement Socratic Questioning

Have you ever asked a toddler to do something and then he or she returns your request with a huff and the demand, "Why?" If you're not careful you can easily get sucked into this game and find yourself held hostage in a never-ending battle of whys. Typically, after a few rounds back and forth with your own little domestic terrorist, you become exasperated and simply reply with a "because I said so." Your sweet angelic toddler is but one enemy of Socratic questioning. The other is the Oracle at Delphi, who claimed Socrates was the wisest man in Greece. When Socrates heard what the Oracle had said, he was caught off guard because surely the Oracle would have to be wiser than Socrates to know exactly how wise Socrates was and name him the wisest man in Greece. This was the fateful beginning of what we now call Socratic questioning.

In the previous chapter, we delved a little bit into Socratic questioning in our attempt at self-discovery. The intent of this chapter is to expand our knowledge as we hear out the arguments of others on our journey to find the "truth."[11] Questioning authority is practically a rite of passage for the majority of individuals as the individual passes through puberty and into adulthood. However, Socrates provides us with the Socratic method of questioning authority so we may find the truth of a particular situation. It's important to note that the Socratic method is not a debate and the individuals participating in the process on any given topic are not there to argue or defend their viewpoint. The participants are present because they want to work together to find out the truth.

To help us get started, think of the Socratic method as a way of thinking that involves three steps. First, we need to define the concept followed by finding exceptions to that definition. Next, presenting those exceptions in the form of a question. In the final step, we should now have a better definition of the concept we are investigating, and the Socratic method will now just repeat itself as it undertakes a new topic.

It is possible to get stuck in the Socratic method as well. Let's suppose that I provide a perfect definition of the concept being investigated using the Socratic method. For many people, that is where the process ends. They have gotten the knowledge from the definition but have missed out on the full understanding of the concept. This is known as rational ignorance.

The Bookfair Exercise

Now, let's use a real example to show how this system really works. In this scenario my five-year-old child came to me after school and excitedly told me there will be a bookfair this week. She wanted to know if I would give her money to purchase books when her class attends their regular library session. Step one: What is a bookfair? A bookfair is a temporary caravan of books that children can buy from at their school. We should all know what a bookfair is now as I've provided the definition, which is step one. But wait! That was a really vague description. You probably still have some questions about bookfairs. Are the books used or new? Are the books age appropriate, and who helps the children pick them out? Can the kids only buy books, or can they spend money on toys and trinkets? Oops. My definition of bookfair left out quite a lot of details. In other words, my definition of a bookfair was lacking in pertinent information.

In order to get a handle on what my child will be purchasing at the bookfair and how much money she will need, we looked over the magazines the publisher sends home periodically. This allowed me to ensure I gave my child the right amount of money for her purchase, and I found the topics of the books she wanted to be appropriate. However, according to Socrates, I don't really understand any of this. I don't really know, and I'm basically ignorant until I can give better, clearer definitions. The consequences of my ignorance are that we know very little. To better understand why we know so little, try defining justice, goodness, truth, beauty, love, or even try defining fish. If you ask me to define a fish, I'm happy to give you a definition, but it's unlikely to be the perfect definition. It won't happen on my first try, that I can guarantee you.

Interestingly, based on what was just said, many people respond and say, "But concepts like values are simply opinions. There's really no truth to them because they are unique to the individual." So there's this idea that the Socratic method just can't get to the truth about some topics. However, the Socratic method still has a lot to offer if that's the case because it helps people think about and identify their true thoughts and opinions regarding their values.

The Justice Exercise

What is justice; exactly what is the definition? We will all have differences of opinions on how to define justice depending on our worldview and the values and norms created by the families and societies that raised us. Some people will see justice as a black-and-white issue, a set of rules that should never be broken. Others will consider the circumstances surrounding the issue as mitigating factors, meaning justice can be more of a gray area for them.

Suppose I believe following the law and making ethically and morally sound decisions is the definition of justice.

Let's consider an example. I work in a supermarket, and I spot one of the customers attempting to steal some items. I report this to the manager on duty, who promptly calls the police. The police arrive at the store, and the man is about to be arrested when I overhear him apologizing to the store manager as he explains he had no way to feed his children right now as he had recently lost his job due to cutbacks. In a show of sympathy for the man's plight, the manager decides not to press charges against the man, just bans him from returning to the store.

In this scenario, I might use Socratic questioning to ask, "If we don't follow through with prosecuting this man, as awful as his situation is, will others believe they can steal from us too?" "Has the man attempted to use one of the foodbanks in the area, and what other resources can we direct him to?" "How do shoplifters affect our bottom line? Because if our store experiences too much shoplifting, our store will go out of business."

I am not trying to be the "bad guy" in this scenario, but these are valid questions someone might use when thinking about how to handle such a difficult predicament. By employing these questions, the idea is to see the bigger picture, but I might also feel guilt, sadness, or sympathy for the man and his family for being in a position that the man felt he had no other option but to steal food. These types of moral dilemmas appear in our day-to-day lives, and using Socratic questioning can help us find our true sense of justice to resolve some very difficult and stressful situations in our lives.

Examples and Exercises

Now it's time to roleplay, and you've been assigned the part of Socrates. Your job will be to ask the questions, just as if this were Athens in the 400s BCE. Your primary goal is to ask questions to better define a term that may be ambiguous or have different meanings to different people. If you think back to the "Bookfair Exercise" in the previous chapter, this exercise will be somewhat similar, except bookfairs are very concrete examples with fairly precise definitions, and we are now going to define abstract concepts with no set definition. The questions that are asked should be specifically aimed at acquiring a solid and cohesive definition of the word we want to define.

Knowledge is Belief

The first term is "knowledge is belief." This is an epistemological theory that in order to have knowledge about a particular topic, a person must also have beliefs about it and vice versa. In Walt Disney's *Dumbo* (1941), Dumbo, a newborn elephant, is delivered to his mother, Mrs. Jumbo, via a stork while riding the circus train to a new location where the circus will be performing. I remember this scene in the movie very vividly for several reasons, but the primary reason is the introduction of the title character. I distinctly recall thinking, as a young child, "Oh, a stork, so that's where babies come from." I later learned it wasn't, nor was it the shopping mall where I wanted to go purchase my sibling a few years later, but I guess that's just as well because they probably wouldn't have let me return her anyway. However, as a small child, I believed babies came from the stork, and that these large white birds flew in your window and deposited infants in your house. I knew that's how I was born. Is that knowledge? Is that real? It was to me at that stage in my life. Because I believed in storks delivering babies, that knowledge was true belief.

Later, as I was so obsessed with the elephants and *Dumbo*, my parents took me to the circus as a special treat, and I got to see the elephants performing in the circus. I was pretty excited and fully expected to see an elephant fly, as that was Dumbo's special talent, attributed to his larger-than-life ears. However, Dumbo was just a make-believe character, so here I learned that while Dumbo was an elephant, not all elephants were Dumbo, and flying elephants were certainly one of a kind, meaning simply believing something was true didn't make it so. This is where the concept that a belief doesn't equal knowledge comes into play. I could believe that storks still deliver newborns to people all over the world and shut all the windows and lock them up tight. However, if I engage in a particular type of activities there's no amount of shutting and locking the windows that will stop the delivery of a newborn baby.

Knowledge is Justified True Belief

Now let's flip this concept upside down and consider a scenario that is an exception to the definition of "Knowledge is true belief." I'm sure you'll have no trouble coming up with an example. The exception might go something like this, "What if I guess the correct answers?" What if I was taking a multiple-choice exam, and I had not prepared adequately by studying, and so simply bubbled in my responses in the "Christmas Tree" pattern. I could still pass the test. In a four-answer, multiple-choice exam, I have a 25% chance of guessing each answer correctly. The odds aren't great, but they are higher than a fill-in-the-blank exam or short-answer exam.

One day I plan on inheriting millions of dollars from a distant relative I have never met. I don't really have a valid reason to think this relative even exists let alone would leave me money, but I like thinking about spending all the money I will one day inherit from this mystery relative. What I am saying is, I can certainly believe in my fancy daydream, but it's impossible for me to know it will actually happen because I don't have any millionaire relatives that I'm aware of. I can't justify these thoughts in reality, my knowledge is based on my gut feeling and nothing more. There is nothing to back up why I am so sure there are great riches in my future.

Here we are again, back at the starting point, but we have made progress. We've retooled our definition of knowledge based on the Socratic method, and what we have now is "Knowledge is justified true belief." As we continue forward the goal remains the same: to reach a better and more accurate definition of knowledge.

The Spirit of Knowledge

A bear is as an animal with fur, right? Let's propose I ask a group of kindergarteners to define a polar bear and they respond by saying it's a big animal with white fur. "What is big exactly? That's a pretty relative term. Big to you may not be big to me at all. And what about rabbits, and dogs, cats, and foxes? There are also snow leopards, and Siberian tigers. Don't they all have white fur too? What sets polar bears apart from these other animals?" These are the types of questions that should force the children to engage their critical thinking skills and start providing a better definition of a polar bear.

According to Plato, I don't know what a polar bear is if I can't define them to the exclusion all other types of bears. In all honesty, that's probably a bit of a stretch for me as I've never been to the Arctic Circle and probably have only seen one in a zoo a handful of times. Sadly, these beautiful animals are a threatened species, though we've seen them navigate into warmer climates to create a hybridized species—the grolar. Like many people, I probably have a stronger relationship with the cute and cuddly idea of polar bears from the Christmas-and-New-Year-holiday Coca-Cola advertisements. If we went to the zoo together I could show you a black bear and tell you that's a black bear or that's a panda bear, but I don't necessarily understand how to individually define them to the exclusion of the others. What I'm doing is really just recognition. Real knowledge comes about when you can discover the spirit of polar bears, the spirit of knowledge.

What is Justice?

One of the primary tenets of the American justice system is that it is better to let ten guilty men go free than to allow one innocent man be convicted. However, in this day and age you can find countless cases that document police corruption and coercion against innocent men and women for the sake of closing a case, revenge, laziness, railroading, or money. Some of these infamous cases include the Central Park 5, the Kids for Cash scandal in Luzerne County Court of Common Pleas in Wilkes-Barre, PA, and Nick Yarris. One prominent example of justice gone wrong, however, is in the case of American serial killer Kenneth McDuff.

McDuff, also known as the Broomstick Killer, had the distinction of being one of twenty death row inmates to be sentenced to death, but was subsequently paroled after his sentence was commuted. McDuff was originally convicted in 1966 and sentenced to death for murdering three teens with a broomstick, though his sentence was commuted to life in 1972 when the Supreme Court of the United States declared the death penalty to be unconstitutional, and he was subsequently released on parole in 1989. McDuff was known to have killed again within three days of his release, and though he was sentenced to death again in 1993 for the murder of six additional women, he is alleged to have more victims who remain unidentified. Many people were outraged when McDuff was identified as the killer in the subsequent six murders as they felt he never should have been released from prison in the first place. The citizens of Texas wanted to know if the original three victims had received justice as McDuff's original death sentence had not been carried out. The families and friends of the six new victims were outraged and asked why the Bureau of Prisons had approved parole for such a vicious murderer when had they not, it would have prevented McDuff from killing again.

Definitions Cont'd

Let's keep pushing onward. A square is a shape with four vertices and four sides. But so are other types of quadrilaterals such as a rhombus, a parallelogram, a rectangle, and a trapezoid. All of the aforementioned shapes meet the previously mentioned definition, but each shape is drastically different, and I could keep going in naming quadrilaterals that meet the definition of having both four vertices and four sides. In our next example, we will define a car as something people drive, but people hardly drive only cars, correct? We drive trucks, SUVs, boats, motorcycles, mopeds, cowboys drive cattle, and you can drive a snowmobile, or a Jet Ski. Almost any motorized vehicle that exists today can be driven, and they are all vastly different. Cars can be electric, gasoline, or hybrid models. There are self-driving models to consider, and many people will even consider the word "car" to be universally interchangeable with some of the other terms listed above, as that is what is used for their everyday transportation. When you really stop and think about all of these little details, Plato's demand for the perfect definition starts to become quite the challenge.

What about love? Do you recall ever becoming so angry with your parents as a child that perhaps, out of anger and frustration and an inability to properly express your emotions, you stomped your feet and yelled "I hate you." when you didn't get your way over something silly or you were disciplined for breaking a rule? How about now as a parent, have you been on the receiving end of that tirade? Have you been obligated to be a proper parent to your child, but out of resentment your child says something like, "You don't love me anymore?" Of course that love didn't just evaporate with the snap of your fingers. You are stepping in to parent your child the same way your parents stepped in to parent you out of love and compassion. But it is possible to fall out of love with a person. The divorce rate is approximately 50%, and that's just among couples who marry. There is a distinct difference between romantic love and parental or familial love.

So now that you've thought about it, do you know what love is? Does it depend on the person? Can you love someone even if you don't like them very much? Is love obligatory in some sense—do I have to love my parents? Now that these questions have started to flow and the process of Socratic questioning is in full swing there is an acknowledgement that there are multiple types of love and thus multiple definitions. Does this work with Plato's requirement for a definition, and if not, how do we rectify that?

The key part of the Socratic method is that it allows us to ask the same questions over and over again in an attempt to define all the difficult and challenging questions we face throughout our lifetime. There is no requirement that we, as humans, reach particular developmental milestones before we employ Socratic questioning. In fact, we can use Socratic questioning on the same topics multiple times on the same subjects as we grow and change throughout our development as social, ethical, and physical beings.

Social scientists such as Art Chickering, Lawrence Kohlberg, and Erik Erikson built their careers and conducted extensive research on the topic of identity development. This research tells us that individuals undoubtedly move through specific stages or can even exist in multiple stages at any given time depending on any number of factors. As a person moves in and out of these developmental stages, their use of Socratic questioning would have them asking deeper, more profound questions and even potentially changing their stances on some issues. This isn't an easy process for anyone, but it isn't meant to be either. Erikson's theory requires that every individual undergo a crisis of two competing issues.

When considering how this might look with other theoretical examples, we can look at

Kohlberg's moral identity development. In a scenario of going to a homeless shelter and helping feed the homeless, someone in the early stages of developing their moral identity might employ questions such as, "How does helping the homeless benefit me? If I help the homeless, will the homeless be able to help me achieve something I need done in return?" On the other hand, a person who is in the later stages of developing their moral identity would ask, "Are there additional things I can do to help the homeless in my city? What do the homeless really need to help them live stable and safe lives?"

Remember, the Socratic method emphasizes that good ideas don't just fall into your lap. They take hard work, and you need to thoroughly think them through. Taking the time to use Socratic questioning on a large variety of topics, as we did here, will help you both develop your skills in asking profound questions but also

make Socratic questioning second nature to you.
Using the Socratic method on your ideas and
opinions will serve to make them stronger, as you
will have already considered many possibilities
when you present them to others.

I'd like to call your attention to a great
video on YouTube called "Socrates and Self-
Confidence" where the content creator compares
the Socratic method to pottery making. Opinions
can be based on reason or complete fluff, and
sometimes it can be a challenge to determine
which opinions are reasonable and which are not.
By employing the Socratic method, you'll be able
to test your opinions to verify that your opinions
are in fact sound and based on something more
than just wild assumption or speculation.

Opinions are basically like a bucket. The
bucket will either hold water or it won't. If your
bucket has a hole at the bottom, it won't be able
to hold water, and the bucket is useless. However,

if the bucket has been kept in good repair and doesn't have a hole in the bottom, the water will remain in the bucket, and you can use the bucket in a variety of ways. The point of this analogy is that many people need to review their opinions and consider all the different aspects of the topic at hand in order to bolster their argument on any specific issue. This is exactly what the Socratic method is designed to help you achieve. By forcing you to think critically about your opinion, you are able to see the proverbial hole in your bucket and plug that hole to provide a sound reason as to where your opinion comes from.

So let's consider two different styles of learning in an average K-12 classroom, lecture- and project-based learning. In lecture-based learning, the teacher typically stands in front of her class and speaks to her class, covering the curriculum material, for the entirety of the learning period. Students are expected to take notes on the material covered and questions are rarely asked. In project-based learning, students are given a project that is designed to demonstrate mastery of certain criteria of the curriculum. Students are then left to figure out how to complete the project either in a group setting or on their own. In this type of learning the teacher will be free to circulate the classroom to answer student questions, and students are freely able to ask questions about their assignment. When a student asks a question, the teacher may even respond with a question as response in an effort to get the student to think critically about the assignment and the material learned in a particular unit.

Do you think one of these types of teaching methods is better than the other? We can argue that project-based learning is certainly more engaging than being spoken at for 45 minutes. Most students would likely experience extreme boredom and their eyes would glaze over about 15 minutes into the lecture. One of the biggest points of using project-based learning is that it does allow students to ask questions to increase their understanding as well as provide teachers with a way to assess student understanding beyond basic testing. We may not call this Socratic questioning specifically in a curriculum, but we are engaging a student's critical thinking skills in these projects and the questioning is one way teachers can see and assess what students know. As I'm sure you can see, Socratic questioning is something that is used very frequently in a variety of settings.

What is Socratic Questioning's Aim?

In this section we will briefly review some of the theories that provide the foundation of the Socratic method. We've already discussed at length how we use Socratic questioning and why it's such a useful skill to develop as it can be used in the average person's day-to-day life, but now let's ask ourselves what we want to do when we choose to use the Socratic method.

So what exactly is the goal of the Socratic method? The answer is a fairly simple one. We want learn "why." By asking strategic and impactful questions, the main purpose of Socratic questioning is to discover new things in an effort to address the question of why. Sometimes topics are easier to address than others. Why does the Earth orbit the sun? Because the gravity of the sun keeps the Earth in its orbit. That's a scientifically factually response. However, trying to address a question such as "Why do we exist?" is much more difficult. There is no factual response for that type of question. These very different types of questions indicate there are actually three differing types of knowledge: know that, know how, and know why.

In the "know that" concept of knowledge we generally are able to pinpoint things we know with certainty and the questions we ask tend to be closed-ended questions to quickly verify the factual response. "I know that grass is green." or "I know that rattlesnakes are venomous." are examples of "know that" knowledge. The types of questions used to acquire this type of knowledge would likely include questions like "Is grass green or purple?" or "Do rattlesnakes kill by venom or constriction?" These questions are simple and have only one correct answer without the ability to extrapolate further.

The "know how" level of knowledge is generally based on skill or the development of skills. The vast majority of people aren't born with the ability to acquire a skill in an instant. It is something that takes time and practice to learn. Think about learning to play a musical instrument. You have to learn to read sheet music, where to place your fingers on the instruments, how to play in proper pitch and time with rest of the band, and how to properly blow through a reed if using a wind instrument. The point is it's a process, and "know how" knowledge requires developing that skill via that process.

The final concept of knowledge is "know why." Suppose we want to know why there has been a cluster of outbreaks in preventable disease in a particular geographic region. There could be any number of reasons. Perhaps there is a group of individuals who have not been vaccinated against the disease due to beliefs or health or access to healthcare. Once we start to ask why, we have opened ourselves up to the primary goal of Socratic questioning.

Let's work through an example of Socratic questioning as it pertains to our final example. When considering explanations and causes (the why) of communicable disease outbreaks, we'll want to organize information and give structure to what we learn. This will allow us to better understand the multiple issues at hand and help us get to the root cause of the issue. For instance, if we ask "Why do we care if there is a public outbreak of the measles?" we will need to think about it terms of the impact on the direct community where these individuals live, other communities the individuals may travel to during the incubation period while they are contagious but not showing symptoms, an increase in deaths of infants and elderly who are more susceptible to communicable disease, the decrease in the protections of herd immunity, and those who could not be vaccinated due to health reasons.

So in this example, the Centers for Disease Control and Prevention would have a vested interest in limiting the amount of exposure individuals with direct contact with this outbreak have with others in an effort to help prevent the spread of the outbreak as well as premature deaths of infants and the elderly. While this particular example is related to measles, we did see a similar response by the CDC in 2014 when Thomas Eric Duncan, a man from Liberia, arrived in the United States with an active Ebola infection that was subsequently passed on to two of his healthcare providers due to the high communicability of the disease. To this day, when going to any doctor or hospital for care, most patients are asked if they have traveled outside the United States within the past 30 days. This question is a direct result of the 2014 Ebola cases. Socratic questioning is being used by healthcare providers to determine whether or not patients might be at risk for having Ebola as doctors do not want these patients exposed to other patients in a waiting area, and doctors also need to ensure they wear the proper protective gear as they treat high-risk patients.

A Group Exercise for Socratic Questioning

Have you ever attended a training or seminar and had the speaker or presenter be less than engaging? Did it feel as if this person was speaking at you for 15, 30, or 45 minutes, and was sucking the very life out of you as you desperately tried not to nod off and embarrass yourself? The best kinds of presentations, meetings, and seminars are those that make you think and want to know more, so you find yourself raising your hand to ask questions or approaching the presenter afterward to find out more. You've fully embraced the Socratic method, and you're thinking critically as you pose your questions to learn "why."

Approaches to Socratic Questioning

1. *The Boot Camp Approach.* The goal of this approach is to break the person experiencing the "boot camp." Imagine you are a brand new private in the army and your boss is a big mean drill sergeant who has it out for you. In all your meetings, your boss drills you constantly, asking question after question until he finally asks one you don't have a response for. Thankfully, we don't see this high-

pressure type of approach too much anymore, which is likely better for everyone's blood pressure.

2. *The Accountability Approach*. Think back to when you were in school. Do you remember when your teacher would call out "Time for a pop quiz"? Whether or not you'd done your reading the night before had a direct impact on how much you sweated it during that quiz. This is the accountability approach in a nutshell. It's simply a checkup on you to verify that you've done the things you should be doing.

3. *The Thinking Approach* is fairly close to the method Socrates practiced when he engaged others in his philosophical

questioning exercises. Here we would see profound questions asked in an effort to get at the knowledge of those being asked to respond as well as their critical thinking process. For example, a law school professor might ask, "Ms. Greene, were the plaintiff's first amendments rights violated when she was prevented from joining other cheerleaders on the football field until after the national anthem had been concluded due to her refusal to stand during the anthem?" The professor will also ask the students to extrapolate beyond their readings to apply theories and principles in advanced ways. For example, "Ms. Greene, does your response change in any way if I tell you that the plaintiff was attending a private university instead of a public state university?"

The Socratic method is an invaluable tool when it comes to learning ethics. Ethical standards can vary by profession, but we start learning right from wrong as very young children. We learn that if we accidentally hurt one of our friends because we were careless and knocked them down we owe our friend an apology. As we develop our own individual sense of identity and norms, we learn to live by a code of ethics and morals set by those who raised us, even if our profession doesn't have a set requirement of ethical practices. However, you will find there are many professions that require individuals to be conscious of their behavior at all times. Some of these professions include teaching, law, medicine, accounting, and nursing, though this is not an exhaustive list. Not all of the issues that arise for professionals will have easy answers that are immediately apparent. The steps below can help you use Socratic questioning to resolve more difficult problems.

1. What is a controversial topic in your workplace? Do you have any policies you feel are outdated, inefficient, or just don't work? Maybe the policy isn't even really controversial. In my workplace there are no provisions for a paid maternity leave policy, and I have long since fought for one due to the financial burdens of caring for a newborn at a time when mothers and infants are most vulnerable.

2. As my workplace is extremely large, the president has provided staff employees with representatives on a committee to tackle this and other types of issues. As I bring this issue to the committee, it will be important for me to focus on the issue at hand, and not allow relevant conversation to veer off course into irrelevant areas. When giving my presentation on the value of a paid

maternity policy, having used the Socratic questioning to form the basis of my reasoning will have been important, but also now during this phase, so will encouraging input from those who are reluctant to participate while simultaneously limiting the contributions of those who are opposed.

3. As the committee discusses this issue it could become confusing as to why our organization would benefit from such a policy. As the person leading this particular conversation, I'll need to be sure I can keep up with all the conversation and organize and analyze the different aspects of what is said. It goes without saying that not everyone is going to agree a paid maternity policy is a good idea, so it will be important for me to make sure my Socratic methodology is on

point, as that will help me have a well-reasoned argument that can help persuade others.

As previously mentioned, the Socratic method is commonly used by law schools when teaching ethics, but it is also used in conjunction with the boot camp method to determine how well students understand the material they've been assigned. In what would probably be close to my worst nightmare, the professor would call on a student at random, and this student is the sacrificial lamb for the moment. The professor peppers the student with questions continuously, even taking the position of a dissenter or critic, which requires the student to defend his or her position. The seasoned law professor keeps challenging the much-less-experienced law student with opposing arguments as the process continues unabated until the student can no longer defend his or her position.

One classic characteristic of a Socratic question is the lack of a single correct answer. The methodology is meant to challenge how you think about things, especially challenging issues, and teach you to ask questions and think critically. One of the easiest and most practical ways to get started with using the Socratic method is to simply ask an open-ended question, ask follow-up questions based on what you learn, and then utilize what you've learned. Remember, this is a learning experience, so don't worry if it takes a couple of tries for you to get used to it. Once you are used to using the Socratic method on a regular basis, the questions will come to you almost automatically.

Using the Socratic Method

I am going to use the Socratic method to challenge whether or not the much more restrictive dress codes for young women in a K–

12 public school setting in comparison to their male counterparts is appropriate. Dress codes for young women versus young men have become more controversial in the past five years or so because dress codes have forbidden young women from showing their shoulders, collarbones, or knees, wearing shorts or skirts at some designated improper level, and the list goes on and on. The reason many schools have communicated these stifling and Victorian-era dress codes is often attributed to the school's male population. The school demands their female student population hide any aspect of their womanhood a man might find pleasing, as that man is simply unable to control his urges, and he is sure to be distracted by the female in her less-than-acceptable attire.

The reasoning and justifications for these stringent policies that objectify women are insulting to both young women and young men. When employing Socratic questioning in relation to dress codes such as this, questions to ask would include:

- Is the administration suggesting that young men are unable to control themselves around young women? Surely young men have willpower, right?

- Are women humans who have the right to dress reasonably and appropriate for the weather? (e.g. men can wear tank tops to school, but women may not) Or are women objects that exist for the purpose of being pleasing to the eye or sexual gratification?

- Why is all the responsibility for "distracting men" placed on women verses teaching men that staring at women is not appropriate or teaching them concentration techniques?

- Does the administration realize that, in the end, under any amount of material, young men and women are still experiencing puberty, and it is far more likely the hormones of their age that is driving their distraction far more than their clothing?
- How does the school rectify allowing cheerleaders or other sports participants to wear uniforms during school spirit days when those uniforms are clearly a violation of dress code?

These are just a few of the questions that have been asked in several of the multitude of real dress code cases that have popped up recently. These issues have included disparaging both male and female students over what they choose to wear. Out of frustration, both students and their parents, many times because the dress codes were not realistic—like trying to find a T-shirt that would not show your collarbones—voiced that the dress codes had gotten ridiculous. Most of the students and their parents felt that the schools were imposing draconian policies, particularly on female students, while male students were treated as if they lacked the mental capacity to accept personal responsibility for their behavior—which the male students were not a fan of either. By asking these questions, often at school board meetings and on news broadcasts, these teens and their parents hoped to bring these issues up for an honest discussion so that reasonable policies could be implemented.

Chapter 3: How to use Socratic Questioning to Persuade Others

The Truth vs. Persuasion

By now you should be able to determine that Socrates' primary purpose when utilizing his technique of asking questions was to get to the truth of a particular ordeal or issue. History tells us that no matter what emphasis the Athenians placed on looks and thereby making Socrates a martyr, Socrates was steadfast in his principles and ethics. He believed in them so unwaveringly it cost him the ultimate price. However, the Socratic method can help us in our modern lives beyond just a search for truth or justice. Socratic questioning can also help give us the tools we need to persuade others.

It's incredibly important to acknowledge from the beginning that using Socratic questioning to persuade others is done in the same fashion Socrates used in Athens all those centuries ago. The persuasive Socratic questioning method is a conversation with those who wish to engage in an examination of their beliefs and ideas. This type of conversation doesn't even have a particular goal in mind. This is different from a persuasive argument, where the goal would be to change the mind of the other party. An example of the persuasive argument between my spouse and I could be:

Spouse: The dog cannot sleep in the bed.

Me: Can you hear the dog crying when he doesn't sleep in the bed? It keeps me up at night. Don't you want me to get a good night's rest?

Spouse: He gets dog hair on the bed, and I don't like that.

Me: If I brush the dog more often and change the bed sheets more frequently, would that make having the dog in the bed more tolerable for you?

Spouse: I suppose we can give it a try. But you have to brush him and change the sheets. If you don't, he can't stay in the bed.

In the above example, I clearly have a primary goal of getting my spouse to allow our dog to sleep with us in our bed. I'm giving him a bit of a guilt trip at first by saying that our dog cries and I can't sleep well, and then I follow that up with agreeing to do some extra work so there won't be so much dog hair in the bed. This isn't a persuasive conversation in the same vein as the Socratic conversation.

In many respects my husband and I do have many Socratic conversations, and sometimes one of us will be persuaded to partially agree with the other's opinions, but many times we have to agree to disagree. For us, this is likely because many of these conversations revolve around "hot button" issues in society today such as politics; legal cases/police behavior; culture, race, and ethnicity; abortion, women's rights, and reproductive rights; immigration; and so many more topics. Be forewarned, these kinds of topics have the potential to explode into an inferno of emotion and can be very devastating to any relationship. These kinds of topics may not be the best to tackle with friends and loved ones unless everyone involved is *willing and able* to set aside their differences on these topics once the conversation is over.

That being said, I am going to present you with what a persuasive Socratic conversation might look like on the topic of breastfeeding in public. In the United States, breastfeeding in public is legal in all 50 states, however, periodically and in more conservative geographical regions, there are news stories referencing nursing mothers being asked to leave public areas (shopping malls, restaurants, pools, playgrounds) for being indecent. In the scenario below let's imagine Jane is a new mother nursing her newborn child in a restaurant while joining her friends Amy and Beth for lunch.

Amy: I don't know how you can do that in public. I would be too embarrassed and think everyone was looking at me.

Jane: I'm feeding my son. He's two months old, and it's perfectly natural. Isn't this what breasts are for? If other people are eating in this restaurant, why is it inappropriate for my child to eat in this restaurant?

Beth: I never thought of it from that point of view. I agree telling women to nurse in a bathroom in unacceptable, but how do you explain what's happening to other children in the restaurant? This is a family establishment.

Jane: But what exactly is visible to the general public? You really can't see anything, can you? I try really hard to be discreet. If it bothers someone, can't they simply look away? How is my child eating in public any different than anyone else eating in public? It makes no logical sense. Do those same parents complain to the publishers about magazine covers they see with cleavage on them? Don't children see those too?

Amy: Aren't you worried someone might call the police?

Beth: That's true. What are you going to do if you get arrested for indecent exposure? You could have a criminal record.

Jane: Breastfeeding in public is exempt from those laws and is legal in all 50 states. I understand this is a personal choice and not everyone is comfortable with it, but it's something I support and believe in.

Beth: Can't you just use a breast pump? Wouldn't that be simpler?

Jane: Not really. Those can take a lot of time, are expensive, and have to be cleaned.

Amy: Well, this conversation has been enlightening. What are we all going to eat?

In this style of conversation between the three women, we see Jane responding to each of Amy's and Beth's questions with statements and questions designed to make the women think about her point of view as a nursing mother. In turn, Amy and Beth are asking questions of Jane that ask her to consider the larger public view. In this conversation, Jane isn't aiming to get Amy and Beth to agree breastfeeding in public is the right decision for them, nor are Amy and Beth telling Jane she should not breastfeed in public. Instead we see Jane expressing her reasons in a persuasive style due to her knowledge on this topic. It's clear she has sound, *justified* reasons for her opinions that she can articulate to others, but Jane is still not, on a proverbial soapbox, preaching that her beliefs are the only acceptable beliefs. That type of conversation would be the antithesis of a Socratic conversation and not at all what we are aiming for.

Seven Key Steps to Effectively and Morally Improve Your Persuasion Skills[9]

Step 1. Mimic Socrates

There's a saying that proposes imitation is the highest form of flattery. When it comes to asking questions and making a point, this is the time to imitate Socrates. Generally, when attempting to persuade others, statements and facts will garner a significant amount of argument. Even if you do thorough research and are fully prepared, someone will challenge the validity of what you're presenting. However, when you use Socratic questioning and make your valid point by asking others to think about the answers to specific questions, participants can't focus on picking apart a statement. They are required to focus on addressing the question.

For example, if you present to a group of engineers with data and reports that the number one hazard on the roadways in your town over the next five years will be unsafe bridges, be prepared for those engineers to suggest that everything from drunk drivers to potholes are actually far more unsafe than the decline in bridge safety. On the other hand, if you ask questions like, "When was the last time the bridges in this area were properly serviced and inspected?" "What is the maximum weight each bridge can handle at any given time, and how much weight is crossing these bridges during the times of heaviest traffic?" and "What is the average cost to bring each bridge up to modern standard versus potential loss of life if the bridges collapse?" the engineers in the room will be focusing on attempting to respond to those questions. Now we can easily see how practicing Socratic questioning will be far more persuasive in assisting us in reaching our goals over simple presentations of statement.

Step 2: A Belief in Their Responses

In addition to being more persuasive, when someone answers the questions you have asked of them they generally will hold their response to be true and accurate. They know they have worked hard and properly researched their response, or know the response is based on education and hard work. This means they are more assured that any of the conclusions they come to from answering one of your questions are correct. They're the person who came to the conclusion in the first place, right?

Step 3: Determine What Facts You Already Assume

When thinking about what questions you want to present to a group, it will be important to think about what facts you already assume to be true. If you notice in the first example regarding the bridges, the questions were framed in a manner that already assumed that the bridges were unsafe and needed to be updated. Therefore, there were no questions that bothered to ask about those kinds of facts. Those kinds of questions would go against the crux of the persuasive argument, so you only want to ask questions that support your position.

Step 4: Make Those Assumptions into Questions

This is a bit of a special skill because you want to make sure, when you turn your assumptions into questions, you do so in a manner that you get the answer you want. Let's say that you work in a school that provides breakfast and lunch to all its students, who are

93

aged from 4 years old to 14 years old. All the children are served the exact same size-portioned meals. Some of the older children have complained the portions are too small and they are often hungry during the day. At the next staff meeting you bring the following questions to be answered:

- Are the daily caloric needs of a 4-year-old and a 14-year-old the same?

- Do we expect children to get the most from a classroom learning environment when they are hungry?

- Do we know that the majority of the students in our school get the majority of their calories here, due to the low socioeconomic status of the school?

The questions above set up the assumptions that demonstrate the need for older children to receive a larger portioned meal for breakfast and lunch. I already know what the answers to these questions are. I don't need to ask them. I am simply strategically phrasing the assumptions in a manner to have others in the staff meeting think about why this will be necessary for older children.

Step 5: Did You Miss an Assumption?

It's also important to realize that when you are going through the Socratic questioning process with the intent of being persuasive that you have to hit all the right chords for your particular group. It's certainly possible to completely miss an assumption on either the emotional or logical level. Taking the example above, I am very likely missing an assumption. Can you tell what it is? How about, don't we care about our students and want to make sure they are receiving proper nutrition?

It's also fully possible for you to assume something incorrectly. Let's say you are requesting that your employer provide a free flu shot clinic at your office so employees can quickly and efficiently receive the flu vaccine this year. You may ask as one of your assumptions, "Don't you care about the health of the employees who work for you?" Your employer may respond by informing you he's far more interested in productivity. So now you'll need to frame your questions around how the flu shot can reduce or prevent time away from the office.

Step 6: What if You're Just Wrong?

It happens, and it is certainly possible that you could have made a mistake and what you thought was an issue really isn't. There's no shame in realizing this and moving on to other areas of your job that really need your attention. In fact, it's a very mature approach. However, if you are still really passionate about whatever it is you were advocating, you'll have to find some other reason for your company to agree with your approach.

Let's look back at the issue regarding portion sizes for older children at the school. Before implementing what was considered to be an overall good idea, the families of the older students were polled and surveyed, and the responses mostly found that students who were still hungry brought additional snacks to school to help curb their appetite and additional portions would be wasteful and were not necessary. However, about 25% of respondents indicated additional portions would be useful.

As a result of the survey and other observances during lunchroom duty over a week period, you decide it would be better to implement a policy whereby students who had unused prepackaged items as well as whole fruit, juice, and milk left over from their breakfast and lunch trays could donate those items back to the school. These items would then be available for any child who wanted an additional item(s) to help complete their meal. This program overall helped reduce waste and did not cost any additional expense.

Step 7: This is Going to Take Time

I do my best thinking in the shower. This is primarily because it is one of the few times during the day when I get the luxury of being completely alone with no interruptions, and if I've planned correctly, I don't have to rush around either. Thinking takes time and so does Socratic questioning. It's not something that is done well with a host of distractions fifteen minutes before I walk into a meeting. Be prepared for persuasive Socratic questioning to be a bit longer of a process. It will take you planning and thoughtfulness, both of which translate into time, for you to develop your questions. However, the payoff is well worth it. The effectiveness of being persuasive and effective at your job and in life will help you reap many rewards and help you reach your most cherished goals.

Examples of When to Use Persuasive Socratic Questioning

A while ago I had an issue with an employer. I was supposed to get paid by my employer once per month, but on this particular month, my employer did not direct deposit the funds into my account as usual. When I inquired as to why, I was informed it was because I had been paid too much money, and I needed to return what I had been paid to my employer. This was such a bizarre situation because I had not been paid at all and my bank confirmed that there was no payment or pending payment from my employer. There was nothing to "pay back" to them, which I said to my employer. My employer then told me I could not be paid until a week later due to this issue, which is illegal in both the state and country I live in.

When I brought up the illegality of these actions and the fact I had done nothing wrong, the person in charge of this issue got angry with me and stated I had no right to say that what was being done was illegal since I had been paid too much. From there, she told others about this situation by stating I was attempting to be paid for hours I did not work, which was not true, and she overall caused a lot of problems for me. In this situation, I thought that knowing my employer's legal obligations, knowing the facts, and being able to show I had not been paid would help me discuss this issue with reason with my employer. Unfortunately, that was not the case. If I had used Socratic questioning to be more persuasive, I might have been more successful at getting this person to see my side of the issue. It honestly didn't matter who was right or wrong in this situation. As soon as my employer felt I was stating they had done something wrong, she shut down and refused to help further. I was forced to go above her to get paid, and I left the company shortly after.

In another example of persuasive Socratic questioning, think about any good salesperson you know. Most highly effective salespeople use Socratic questioning techniques in order to persuade you to buy whatever product it is they sell. Let's look at the classic example of a car salesman. The last time I purchased a car, I recall being asked questions such as the following:

- Are you looking for a new car for your family?
- About what price range do you want to stay in?
- Are you planning to trade in the car you drove into the lot today?
- Where do you want your monthly payments to be?

- What kinds of features are important to you?
- Does the car have to be an SUV or sport wagon?
- Will you be financing the car you purchase?

Those are just some of the questions I can recall over a year after the fact. As you can see, there are some questions that assume that I am definitely going to be purchasing a car and that it will be from that specific dealer. The questions about financing, trade-in, and monthly payments allow the dealer to provide an estimate of how much I will be spending on a particular car (i.e. the salesman isn't showing me BMWs when I can only afford a Kia). My answers to these questions allow the salesman to show me the best options he has in stock that meet these qualifications and persuade me that these are the best choices in terms of making a final purchase.

Another question that is commonly asked in sales is "Don't you deserve it?" or "Don't you want your family to have the best?" This is a very persuasive question and it's a trap that a lot of people will fall into because when it comes to their family, they do want the best. They want their children to be protected by dual-side airbags or to have that entertainment system in the back so they can watch movies on road trips. It's important to remember that while you may use these tips, you are also aware of them potentially being used on you as well.

There is a reason that the Socratic method has stood the test of time over the past 2400 years. It's because it's highly effective. Perhaps the Oracle at Delphi was correct, and Socrates was indeed the wisest man in Greece. The next time you need to pull someone over to your side, especially over an important issue, use Socratic questioning to persuade the other person over to your way of thinking rather than getting into a battle over who is wrong and who is right.

Examples of Persuasion Cont'd

When my son, David, was about halfway through fourth grade we got a nasty surprise in the form of his academic progress report. It showed he was failing three out of his four courses in school. An immediate parent-teacher conference the next business day further revealed he had developed an alarming habit of "losing" his worksheets so he wouldn't have to complete them. My son's grades were terrible, but I wasn't quite sure how to deal with it, because this was the first time anything like this had ever happened.

Did I punish him and take away all of his privileges? No television, no Nintendo, no movies until his grades came back up? What about bribing him? I was fully aware that some parents in our social circle bribed their kids into getting good grades. These parents gave their kids $20 for every A, $10 for every B, and $5 for a C. I personally was totally against that. I could threaten him over any number of things: canceling his upcoming birthday party, prohibiting any playdates with friends, pulling him from his extracurriculars. I was at a bit of a loss, really, but then I thought about some of the counseling literature I've previously read. Dr. Michael Pantalon, senior research scientist in emergency medicine at Yale School of Medicine, in his book *Instant Influence: How to Get Anyone to do Anything—Fast,*[10] discusses asking two irrational questions to effectively deal with motivation issues.

When David returned from school that afternoon, I decided to put Dr. Pantalon's methods to work. I asked him, "David, on a scale of one to ten, one being not ready at all and ten being let's sit at the table this instant and get them done now, how ready are you to work on your assignments and complete your missing work?" I'd collected at least a month of missing assignments from his teachers so it was doubtful David would shout out with a nine or ten, but he also knew he had messed up by letting this happen, so he knew I expected him to start working toward rectifying this issue. David responded with a three.

The first instinct as a parent is to roll your eyes and inform your child, who gives you that ridiculously low number, that he's at a ten and to get his pencil because his bottom would be glued to the chair until his assignments were completed, but don't do that. Ask him another irrational question. "Why are you a three? Why aren't you a two or a one?" Now David explains to me all the other things he has going on in the world. He has a spelling test in two days he needs to study for, and there is karate practice that night after dinner. He wants to take a little break when he gets home from school because he's been there all day. He wants a little time to watch television or play a videogame. He doesn't have much time to do the extra work between studying for spelling, his regular homework, going to karate, and doing his regular chores at home like loading the dishwasher and feeding the dog.

I tell David I'll take care of feeding the dog and doing the dishes, but that he isn't going to karate. Taking David out of karate for the evening isn't a punishment, and I explain that to him. It's simply to relieve whatever pressure he's feeling with so much on his plate. I also let him take a 15-minute break and send him outside to play with a snack. By asking David the two irrational questions, I've learned why my son has been losing his assignments this term. He has too much on his plate and he hasn't really learned the skills of time management.

What if David had said he was a one? Well, that can be a little trickier, but it's really important information to have. If David had told me he was at a one when it came to completing his missing assignments, I would have asked him what it would take to get him to the next level—a two. Based on how our conversation went with him at a three, I would expect David to let me know he needed more study time than his current schedule allowed. He may have gone so far as to ask not to go to karate and to skip some of his chores. It's important to remember that in this scenario my most important goal is to understand why my child is suddenly having this issue. By applying the original Socratic principles, we can get to that information quickly, and David's grades started to bounce back almost immediately.

Chapter 4: Using Socratic Questioning with Cognitive Behavior Therapy

Socratic Questioning in Therapeutic Settings

To be clear from the beginning of this chapter, I am not a therapist, and I am not representing myself as one either. This chapter is simply to discuss the many uses of the Socratic method for those who are therapists or who seek the services of a therapist. Counseling and therapy services can be priceless when it comes to helping you navigate a particular issue or difficult period in your life. There are many types of therapy such as marital therapy, therapy for post-traumatic stress disorder (PTSD), child counseling, individual counseling, counseling for aging populations, and drug and alcohol dependency counseling. Basically, if you have an issue you need to talk through with someone, there is a therapist out there who can help you.

However, it can take time for the patient-doctor relationship to develop enough trust that the patient is willing to divulge the full reason they are seeking therapy. It's not uncommon for a patient to state they are seeking therapy for one reason, but later reveal they are really seeking therapy for a related, but deeper, issue. An example of this might be a patient who asks to discuss their lack of organization skills as this has had a significant impact on their life. Later, the patient may reveal that they are, in actuality, a hoarder whose home is overrun by junk and garbage and Adult Protective Services has been called in to insist the hoarded home be cleaned up or the home will be condemned. Socratic questioning used in therapy sessions can help both the therapist and patient identify the true purpose of therapy sooner rather than later.

Admitting these kinds of deeply personal things about yourself is not easy, and in many cases, they are not the kinds of things you would want to share with your closest friends and family either. However, a good therapist can use cognitive restructuring in an effort to help you change your problem behaviors in order to have a more positive impact on your life. According to Therapist Aid, "Cognitive restructuring refers to the process of challenging and changing irrational thoughts. Socratic questioning is one technique to encourage this process. Therapists use Socratic questioning verbally by asking probing questions about their clients' irrational thoughts. As clients improve their awareness of irrational thoughts, they can begin to consciously question their own thoughts."[11]

By using Socratic questioning in therapy sessions, the therapist's goal is to assist the patient in determining which thoughts are irrational and subsequently lead the patient down a path of problem behaviors. The therapist then works with the patient to help them identify these thoughts on their own, so the individual can prevent these behaviors before they even begin.

How to Use the Socratic Method Effectively in Therapy Sessions

Foundations of Cognitive Therapy

The foundations of cognitive therapy can be found in cognitive theory, which means that there is a relationship between the body, emotions, behavior, and a person's surroundings.[(12)] In cognitive theory, these parts of ourselves work together and create meaning in our lives, but because of how these elements interact, changes depending on the different contexts of our situations. They impact how our goals will change as well. It's also possible that thoughts and beliefs that are not true, but instead reflect cognitive bias or misrepresentation, will also affect meaning. What this means is that in cognitive therapy, there is a singular explanation for changes in thoughts and behaviors and how they assist with problems the patient is coping with.[12]

Another tenet of cognitive therapy is case conceptualization. This is a skill possessed by the therapist whereby the therapist examines how the emotions, behavior, environment, physical make-up, and thought process all work and relate to each other in several different contexts and with various diagnoses.[12] The aim of therapist is to determine what interventions will be most successful for the patient, while also ensuring the interventions are implemented in a way the patient will find respectful.

Collaborative Empiricism

When a person goes to therapy for any reason, who is responsible for ensuring that the patient reaches their goals? Maybe you think it is the therapist, who is being paid for their services. Perhaps you think it is the patient, who has the dysfunctional behaviors in the first place. In cognitive therapy, the concept of collaborative theory states that both the patient and the therapist must work together to achieve the goals of therapy. On one hand, the therapist needs to be engaged in asking insightful, well-thought-out, and sensitive questions in an effort to gather data as to why the patient is engaging in the undesirable thoughts or behaviors. On the other hand, the patient will need to test out the hypothesis the therapist develops from the answered questions. It is up to the patient to take on this piece of work from therapy. It's also important that the therapist respect and appreciate the patient's autonomy during this process, as it will continue to foster a trusting relationship between the patient and the therapist.[12]

Guided Discovery

Guided discovery is when the therapist assists the patient with the discovery of their collection of beliefs and opinions.[12] In cognitive therapy, the therapist focuses on information the patient discusses during their therapy sessions. In guided discovery, rather than offer a patient insight to solving a particular problem, the therapist uses Socratic questioning to bring the patient's thoughts into hyper focus. By focusing on cognitions, the therapist is able to help the patient pinpoint beliefs and opinions that may be based on incorrect information and have the patient consider other options that may improve the patient's circumstances.[12] The therapist is able to do this by employing Socratic questioning. When the patient answers the therapist's questions, the answers should be in contrast to the patient's current beliefs.

The Socratic method is a significant part of guided discovery because it allows the therapist to engage patients in order to learn useful information and then process that information in a way that benefits the patient's therapy. Like other types of Socratic questioning, it's important that the therapist not engage with the patient as if they were in an interview. The tone of the questions and overall sessions should be conversational, just as if you were still playing the role of Socrates back in chapter two. Again, a respect for the autonomy of the patient should be honored as it has a significant impact on the relationship between the therapist and patient.

What Socratic Questioning Is Not— Especially in Therapy Sessions

I hope this section has thoroughly stressed to you the value of the collaborative relationship between the therapist and patient and how the use of both collaborative empiricism and guided discovery rely on both individuals in order to be successful. Now it's important to emphasize that it's possible to use Socratic questioning incorrectly. Specifically, by disputing your patients' responses and turning them into a "right or wrong" type of situation. Some therapists who practice this style of questioning refer to it as "Socratic disputing."[12]

The Socratic method is distinctly different from an argument or a debate. It's important to remember this method relies on the technique of a conversation. We are not aiming to change an individual's mind. We are aiming to encourage individuals to think critically about their beliefs and behaviors and how irrational thoughts are having a negative impact on those beliefs and behaviors. Not all therapists practice cognitive behavioral therapy and thus they won't rely on the Socratic method, but those who do will focus on the collaborative process called for in this style of counseling.

Making the Most Out of Socratic Questioning

In addition to maintaining a collaborative stance when working with clients, it is also important that clients feel safe while in therapy sessions. One way this can be implemented is rather than engaging in the "Socratic disputing" mentioned above, instead, be curious. Being inquisitive and asking questions over assuming you already know a patient's collection of beliefs and opinions is likely to lead you to a true discovery. If you skip this step, you may very likely skip a critical piece in the client's thought process that is contributing to their dysfunctional behavior.

You may have heard the phrase, "You shouldn't have asked the question if you didn't already know the answer." However, in cognitive therapy, therapists are actively encouraged to ask questions that will give them new information on their clients' lives and thought processes. This allows them to enter the guided discovery phase earlier in an effort to find viable solutions for the patient's irrational thoughts and dysfunctional behavior.

Example of Socratic Questioning in a Therapy Session: Family Issue

Therapist: How are you, Eve? So, today we're talking through a situation where you feel as if your mother-in-law ignored you. You said you said something to her, right? And you kind of identified this thought or this assumption that she doesn't like you? So, I thought we'd maybe do a little bit of a dialogue back and forth. I could ask you some questions about what happened and how you feel about the situation. This is called Socratic questioning. Is that okay with you if we dive into this?

Eve: That's fine.

Therapist: Okay. So, in relation to this idea here, this situation, you think your mother-in-law's point of view is that she doesn't like you.

Eve: Yeah.

Therapist: Is that right? So, do you want to round that out any more? What else might she thinking?

Eve: Well, my husband and I just got married, and we've been living with my in-laws for about a month, just until his new job starts in a few weeks. I walked into the house a few days ago and said hello and asked her if she needed anything, but she completely ignored me. It was like I wasn't even there. So, you know, I'm thinking, "Yeah, she doesn't like me, she's kind of a jerk."

Therapist: Okay. So you feel your mother in law doesn't like you. And you also think she's kind of a jerk.

Eve: Yes. Exactly.

Therapist: Right. Which one feels stronger, more accurate? Should we think about it right now?

Eve: She doesn't like me.

Therapist: "She doesn't like me." You're pretty focused on that today. So, if you think about that idea in your mind, what assumptions are you making? Are you making assumptions about how your mother-in-law feels about you based on a single interaction?

Eve: I'm assuming… because she wouldn't acknowledge me that she doesn't like me.

Therapist: Okay.

Eve: So, that's an assumption.

Therapist: Right. So you see a link that acknowledging you means someone likes you and not acknowledging you means that they don't.

Eve: That's true, when you phrase it like that.

Therapist: Okay. Anything else?

Eve: It's possible she didn't hear me. She was reading a book when I came in so she should have heard me, but she could have been really focused on her reading.

Therapist: That's a significant assumption that she actually heard you.

Eve: I guess I'm assuming she did because I was standing pretty close to her.

Therapist: Okay, so you've made a couple of assumptions here. One assumption is that if someone doesn't acknowledge you it means they don't like you and vice versa. There's also the assumption that your mother-in-law heard you in the first place.

Eve: Right.

Therapist: There are a couple of things that stand out here. Based on your assumptions, you've come to the conclusion your mother-in-law doesn't like you. Do you have any proof or evidence that suggests she doesn't like you?

Eve: The evidence would be the lack of acknowledgement. I don't know, I guess other times, do you mean like... show other points where she ignored me?… I can't exactly remember. Sometimes she can be a little cold toward me.

Therapist: Okay. Do you have any other reasons to think that your mother-in-law doesn't like you?

Eve: She doesn't go out of her way to include me in things.

Therapist: Okay. That's something to consider, isn't it?

Eve: Yes.

Therapist: And so as far as you're concerned, after you were ignored, you decided your mother-in-law must not like you.

Eve: That's correct.

Therapist: Why did you come to that conclusion? What made you think that was the best option?

Eve: I hope I'm wrong, but it just seems like the evidence points that way.

Therapist: Okay, but given the assumptions we've discussed and the overall lack of evidence, are there other viewpoints or other conclusions you could have settled on?

Eve: I could have looked at it differently. Like I said, she might have just been absorbed in her book. She's an avid reader. Or maybe she was stressed out and didn't realize I was there. She could have been tired from work too.

Therapist: Those are all possible reasons why she may not have responded to you. So why, when we have all these viable reasons for why your mother-in-law didn't acknowledge you, did you settle on the reason that it was because she didn't like you?

Eve: I didn't think of all the other reasons.

Therapist: But you are now? What is it that you're thinking?

Eve: That perhaps I judged too quickly, and I should have been more open-minded.

Therapist: Now go back to your first inclination, "She doesn't like me." When you think that and you hang on to that as the reason your mother-in-law didn't acknowledge you, how does it make you feel?

Eve: I feel depressed and lonely. Like I can't talk to my mother-in-law any longer.

Therapist: Okay, and what about when we consider the other possibilities for why you weren't acknowledged? How do those possibilities make you feel?

Eve: If one of them was the real reason my mother-in-law ignored me, I'd know it wasn't about me and I'd feel relieved. I would feel happy, I suppose, because everything I was worried about would be gone.

Therapist: Do you think having this conversation has helped you consider alternative reasons for why your mother-in-law might not have responded to you?

Eve: Absolutely, it's really made me look at what happened and think about things differently.

Therapist: And now that you're considering that you weren't purposefully ignored, how does that make you feel on an emotional level?

Eve: Surprised. It makes me wonder why I didn't think of these things. I just immediately latched onto the idea that my mother-in-law hated me now that I had married her son. A part of me still thinks that is probably true, but just thinking through all the other possibilities has me doubting what I thought I knew with certainty an hour ago.

Therapist: That's the intention of cognitive therapy. We'll work together to get you to start wondering about different conclusions and considering different possibilities. As you think through different problems and the solutions and conclusions of those problems, we'll see how your decisions make you feel.

Eve: That sounds like a plan.

Example of Socratic Questioning in a Therapy Session: Dating and Resiliency

Therapist: How are things going on the dating front?

Tom: Not particularly well. I've gone on a lot of first dates. I think they go well, but when I try to ask the women out for a second date, they don't answer my calls or return my messages or texts. I've pretty much decided to stop dating.

Therapist: That a pretty significant decision. We should probably talk about it. When did you make this decision?

Tom: Last Tuesday. I tried to call the woman I took out on a date on Friday night to let her know I'd had a good time and to see if she wanted to go out again, and she said she just wasn't interested.

Therapist: So, when your most recent date stated she wasn't interested in continuing to see you, is that when you gave up hope?

Tom: Yeah. I remember thinking I couldn't take any more rejection. I've had a lot of dates over the past year since Allison and I broke up, and they never go anywhere. It makes me feel like a social pariah.

Therapist: I can imagine that's been difficult for you, especially reentering the dating scene after a long-term relationship. Let's see if anything positive came out of dating for you.

Tom: I can't really think of anything. It's been almost a year since I started dating again, and I don't think I've made to any second dates, let alone anything even resembling a solid relationship.

Therapist: How many dates do you estimate you've been on since you started dating again?

Tom: I don't know. An average of one a
week for the last year, so 52… I guess.

Therapist: I can see that you've taken dating
             really seriously and put in a lot of
             effort. But I think the important
             question here is whether or not it's
             worth it to continue dating. How
             many dates do you think the
             average person has to go on in
             order to find the person they want
             to be in a relationship with?

Tom: I think I'd probably imagine it
could be 25 or 30, but I suppose it could take
more.

Therapist: So considering that information,
             does 52 dates seem wholly
             unreasonable? Do you know
             anyone who dated many more
             people than 25 or 30 or even 52?

Tom: Well, I have a buddy who was a bit of a playboy. I'd assumed he was a confirmed bachelor as he was dating a different woman every time I saw him, but lo and behold he met the love of his life one day and settled down with her pretty quickly after they met. He'd been dating around for years before he met her.

Therapist: Really? That sounds like an important piece of information. What if your friend had come to you after a year of dating and said he wasn't going to date any longer because he hadn't met "the one" yet?

Tom: I probably would have told him he was being silly and that it takes time to meet the right person. It's kind of like a needle in a haystack, and not to give up.

Therapist: I think that sounds like reasonable advice. I know it's hard to keep that kind of thing in mind, especially after several disappointments. Do you think your advice also applies to your situation?

Tom: I suppose it does.

Therapist: So what can you do to help you keep this in mind so you don't get discouraged about dating in the future?

Tom: I suppose I could write a note to myself and keep it on my cellphone so it will be easy to pull up. If things don't work out after future dates, the note can remind me that searching for someone to share your life with is like searching for a needle in a haystack and not to be discouraged if this person didn't work out because there are plenty of fish in the sea.

Therapist: That's an excellent idea. So now let's talk about some reasons why you may not be getting acceptances when you ask women out on second dates.

Tom: Good deal.

Applying Socratic Questioning to Thoughts[13]

Although it may not sound difficult, you may be surprised to find out that it is rather challenging to apply the Socratic method to the thoughts and ideas that enter your brain. That's because you think these ideas and thoughts so quickly there's rarely any time to consider them. However, it goes without saying that there are times when you will sit down and ponder some questions or more important thoughts in your life. In an exercise provided by Therapist Aid, there are questions anyone applying the Socratic method can use. In addition to answering the questions asked below, make sure you elaborate on your answer and indicate why or why not.[17]

It can be very helpful for both a therapist and patient for a patient to think critically on a particularly difficult topic and thoughtfully apply the Socratic method in writing by asking themselves the questions below. The first thing we need to do is select a thought or idea we want to examine through Socratic questioning. In the example below, we will pick up where the prior example left off in Tom's therapy session and then address the questions as if Tom were responding.

Thought to Be Questioned: I cannot successfully carry any first dates into a second date.

What is the evidence for this thought? Against it?
I have been on approximately 52 dates in the past year, and none of them have led to a second date despite my attempts to contact my dates within a reasonable time period to let them know I enjoyed the date—and all indications point to they also enjoyed the date.

Am I basing this thought on facts or on feelings?
Probably both. It is factual that none of my first dates have led to second dates, but there is an emotional component of rejection involved after each rejection. It's possible that after a certain amount of rejection that a certain level of bitterness and resentment was communicated to later dates and I did not realize this.

Is this thought black and white, when reality is more complicated?

This is a tough question to address. On one hand, the response is a yes or no response, but when dealing with all the issues of dating and the emotions and thoughts that go into it, it's definitely a complicated issue.

Could I be misinterpreting the evidence? Am I making any assumptions?

I don't think so. Sure, if we were talking about a smaller group of women, I would say that's a definite possibility. However, being that this has happened every single time, it's hard to ignore that something is going on. I am not saying that in each case the issue was me, but it's concerning.

Might other people have different interpretations of this same situation? What are they?

Maybe? I guess so? The women might have a completely different interpretation, but asking them would be awkward, and nobody really wants to give out that kind of information.

Am I looking at all the evidence, or just what supports my thoughts?

This is hard to address. I probably don't have all the evidence because 50% of it walked away when the date ended, so I can really only go on what's left over at the end of the date. Truthfully, I don't know why the dates didn't work out, and I have to remember that there were definitely some cases where I didn't pursue additional dates because *I* wasn't interested. I think that's the first time I've remembered that fact.

Could my thought be an exaggeration of what's true?

I think this exercise has just helped me point out that I was exaggerating at least a little bit. Sure, I've been on about 50 dates, but I haven't pursued 50 different women for a second date. This is really the first time that I've sat down to remember that there were many times I wasn't interested in going further with dates either.

Am I having this thought out of habit, or do the facts support it?

I don't necessarily think the facts support it the way I thought they did. I think I may have just been really psyched up about the possibility of developing relationships with some of the women who subsequently rejected me. I was way too hasty in my thought process, and when it didn't go anywhere the rejection was worse than I expected.

Did someone pass this thought/belief to me? If so, are they a reliable source?

No, it's just that I was in a long-term relationship with my previous girlfriend for five years, and I enjoyed that. I would like to have that kind of relationship again, and I've been doing everything I can to rush, rush, rush into that without realizing that maybe this isn't something you can rush.

Is my thought a likely scenario, or is it the worst-case scenario?

I think my thought is probably a manifestation of my biggest fear, which is being alone. I've always wanted to settle down and have a family. I don't know if it's a worst-case scenario exactly, but I would say that the more rejections I experienced, the more pressure at dating and finding the right person I felt.

In the above exercise, we can now see Tom identify that while he's had a lot of dates over the past year, he has not, in fact, tried to pursue all of them for second dates. We get much better insight, but most importantly so does Tom, about why he may be failing in his dating life. Now he can take this exercise back to his therapist, and together they can work collaboratively on strategies to help him be more successful at dating again.

Chapter 5: How to Ask Better Questions in Organizations

How to Effectively Use Socratic Questioning as a Leader

Being a leader can be extremely challenging, and those challenges can increase when leadership changes or leaders attempt to change the culture of their business. This is a paradigm shift for the organization, and acquiring the "buy-in" from the organization's employees can be a challenge. Let's suppose this employer wants its employees to step up their performance to meet specific goals. As a reward, employees who meet performance goals will receive monetary bonuses, and the focus of the organization will shift to focus more on the staff's performance versus the number of hours they put in at the office.

The leaders at the organization can announce these changes to their staff in several different ways. They can simply announce these changes and expect the staff to all jump on board, or they can apply Socratic questioning to pump up and excite the staff about the new changes. Let's see how that might look.[14]

Leader: Can our business meet and exceed its sales goals?

Staff: You bet we can.

Leader: If we meet our goals, should we be eligible for bonuses?

Staff: Absolutely.

Leader: What if one of us is really

efficient, and teaches us how reach our goals with less work, meaning we don't have to spend as much time in the office?

Staff: That would be awesome!

Leader: Is it just as good as working a full, forty-hour week to achieve the same results?

Staff: Definitely.

Leader: How would we factor that into how bonuses are calculated?

Staff: It should be based on overall performance and reaching sales goals.

In this example, the leader has brought the staff around to a conclusion as to how bonuses will be calculated by having them answer pre-planned questions. With that process, the leader has also acquired buy-in from the staff and excited them about the possibilities of future bonuses that await them. The staff now feel a part of the decision to restructure the organization's culture over having such a momentous change simply mandated to them.

One of the bigger challenges a leader can face is connecting each employee to the mission and goals of the organization. Suppose the purpose behind your organization is to provide lasting homes to stray animals in the area where you live. As the director of this organization, you attend meetings and fundraise to the public explaining the things your organization does to achieve its goals. You work with veterinarians who help assess your animals and make sure they are healthy enough to be adopted, but also spay and neuter the animals so they can't contribute to pet overpopulation. You work with several people who assess the potential owners to ensure they are good fits for the animals they want to adopt, so you aren't placing animals who are skittish in a home with small children or larger animals who need space to run in an apartment living situation.

But what about those people who come in daily to clean up after the animals? Or help in situations when there is no hope and the animal has to be euthanized because it's unsuitable for any home or because the injuries it has suffered are too severe? How do you explain the mission and goal of your organization to those who may not get to see how their role impacts the bigger picture? As a quality leader, you should be able to not only see the value of all your employees, but also help them see the value and need of what they do in your organization. One of the ways you can do this is by asking "how" and "why."[14] Let's use our animal shelter example to address the questions below with our employee who helps us keep the animal cages clean and the animals walked and fed.

Director: Why do the dog and cat cages need to be cleaned regularly?

Staff: So the animals are able to reduce their stress levels, stay healthy, and maintain proper standards of care.

Director: What does having animals that are healthy and less stressed achieve?

Staff: Those animals are ready for adoption, and people who come in to adopt those animals will see that they are healthy and happy.

Director: Why is that important?

Staff: Because then the animals are more likely to be adopted, which opens up space for other animals that may otherwise have to go to another shelter.

Director: Why don't we want animals to go to other shelters?

Staff: The majority of shelters in our area euthanize animals due to the shortage in availability of space. So, the more animals we adopt out to good homes, the more space we have for others who need it.

By using the Socratic method, this leader was able to help this employee pinpoint the crucial role they play in the overall functioning in the organization. It's rare that an employee can take their job description and their company's mission and find some way that the two align. If you, as a leader, can show them how they play a pivotal role in the success of the organization and that they aren't simply pushing paper around a desk, you have the ability to connect to your workforce in a way that money cannot. People feel differently about their jobs when they are doing something they believe in. I'm not suggesting salary isn't important, but you'll likely never find me working for a company that produces something I oppose on a moral or ethical level.

How to Make Better Decisions

Can you name one thing that Steve Jobs, Bill Gates, and Mark Zuckerberg have in common? They are all college dropouts. That's hardly news these days, but despite leaving school in the middle of their degrees, these men went on to become incredibly successful entrepreneurs, and they are hardly the only ones. Some people will leave school because it just isn't right for them, but some people leave because they just aren't getting much from it.

One of the criticisms faced by education today is that it doesn't "teach" thinking skills at all. In fact, education has really become the memorization of dates and facts to be recalled for a test and then simply forgotten once a grade is earned. The criticism is that people no longer know how to analyze and synthesize information at all because they were never taught those skills, and as a result most people are simply able to reiterate thoughts and ideas they've heard on the news from their favorite pundit or television program.

One of the goals of cognitive neuroscience is to examine how individuals learn and what factors influence thinking, learning, and memorization. One way researchers have been able to study this is through simulations. Today, we have access to advanced computer simulations that allow us to challenge an organization's leader with the same type of issues and concerns that might truly be faced by an organization. These simulations allowed researchers to see the thinking process of a leader as they confront problems within the organization, which often resorted to guessing and poor decision-making, even when the leader was provided with more supportive resources. The consensus amongst the researchers was that perhaps decision-making might improve if it was approached collaboratively and a team was making organizational decisions versus a single person, as decision-making seemed too large a task for a single person to take on alone.

Now let's look at an example. I work for a big research-based university, and the head of the department has tasked me with growing the graduate program by 45%. That's quite a task, and I sit down with faculty and staff to get input on how to achieve this. I ask, "What areas do we need to focus on to grow the graduate program?" The faculty respond that more programs are needed in specific high-volume areas and that we will need more faculty to teach those programs. The staff state that we will need to recruit students for those programs, but also increase student populations in current programs, meaning enlarging current class sizes, leading back to the issue of needing more faculty. Also, as more students enroll, the staff will need to be increased to ensure a proper dispersion of services.

Next, I ask for all of us to come together to map out a timeline for when things will need to take place. We know certain things, like creating new programs and hiring new faculty, are lengthy practices, taking 12-18 months on average. In working with variables we have control of now, we look at admitting 20% more students into our current programs as not all students elect to matriculate. In five years, we find that we have successfully started two new programs, hired four new faculty members, increased our enrollments by 50%, and hired a full-time staff member to take on the additional workload affiliated with the additional students.

How did we do this? How did we lead and succeed in our growth goals in a five-year period? We did this by asking questions meant to get at the root of the issues we were facing. We purposely involved multiple groups and played on their expertise and knowledge to benefit us in our overall goal. We asked what their subcomponent of the graduate program needed to be successful and increase growth overall, and we delivered on those needs. Furthermore, we made them part of the growth process and created buy-in to our goals. We did the exact same things with staff. We did not want the groups competing against one another for perceived resources. Instead, by bringing everyone together, we put everyone on the same playing field and made it clear this was a shared goal. No one needed to fight or argue over the importance of their role. It was clear from the beginning we would work together to meet the department head's expectations.

Think about this style of leadership and this approach for a moment. Would you enjoy it if your organization shifted its thought process and started using Socratic questioning? Think about how inspired you might be by a good supervisor who knew how to motivate those who worked with them. Instead of leaving staff meetings feeling as if your entire job hinged on your ability to reach a sales goal by the end of the month, you might leave that meeting inspired to meet that goal quickly and efficiently. You might find yourself asking, "How can I help others on my team succeed?" "How can I motivate others to be successful?" or "What does my team really need?" This is a far cry from worrying only about yourself and your individual role. As you develop more comfort and expertise with Socratic questioning, you may find that you start shifting into the role of leader yourself.

Socratic Questioning at Work: Alpha Consulting Case Study[15]

In this case study, an IT value management company, Alpha Consulting, has come to a crossroads within three years of launching its business due, in part, to rapid expansion. The business was originally started in the United Kingdom but has subsequently expanded into continental Europe, America, and Asia Pacific. With these expansions, the role of the company changed somewhat in each of these locations, depending on their individual needs. At this time, the company is questioning those decisions and also questioning some of its core principles, such as staying separate from vendors and picking IT value management over business value management.

The firm held an annual globe planning meeting each year, attended by the firm's twelve partners. Due to all the changes and issues mentioned above, the following questions were set to be addressed:

- How do other professional services firms approach knowledge management?
- How does this firm's approach to knowledge management relate to their competitive strategy?

Once everyone came to the table, the meeting facilitators began a process of Socratic questioning to determine a knowledge management strategy for their firm. The facilitators used the Socratic method in this case to draw on the experience of the partners at the consultancy firm. Because the firm was quite young, many of the partners had experiences that had taken place at firms where they had worked prior to being employed with Alpha.

During the discussion of the continental European situation, the partners engaged in a lively conversation of whether or not it wanted to be in the business of providing solutions and how, if they maintained their focus on IT value management, they would be able to grow at their expected rate. During the discussion of the fourth partner's experience, the group decided they no longer wanted to continue with the remaining experiences and decided to focus on creating a set of principles for knowledge management purposes. The remainder of the session saw the development of nine such principles.

Socratic Questioning at Work: Beta-Telco Case Study[15]

In this case study, we look at Beta-Telco, a Chilean telecommunications service provider. At the time of the case study, Beta-Telco, whose focus was on providing services in the corporate sector, provided services to about 60% of the market. Beta-Telco also provided services via mobile services under another subsidiary, but that company was not discussed as part of this case study. Due to its dominance in the market, the leaders at Beta-Telco determine they will need to offer new products to continue to grow. Beta-Telco begins to offer IT outsourcing services as one of its products.

As part of the changes affiliated with this new service, Beta-Telco did not immediately implement the organizational changes that would be needed to adequately provide for them, opting instead to appoint ad hoc committees on an as-needed basis. However, as the demand for these services grew and knowledge management clearly came to an area that was lacking, the leadership decided to create a knowledge management network that focused on six Communities of Practice (CoP).

The plan was for the first CoP, Technological Convergence at Beta-Telco, to be built as a pilot, and then the remaining five CoPs would be built based on what was learned when building the first CoP. While the CoPs were designed with the idea of operating in a virtual space, the Convergence CoP did meet monthly during the first five months of its existence. During the third meeting, the CoP's leader initiated Socratic questioning by asking, "What positive and negative experiences have we had in delivering this service to clients?" The question was designed for members of the CoP to look back at previous experiences in Beta-Telco when providing this service, though one example was from a different company, so they could be analyzed.

The results of the CoP critically reviewing, analyzing, and thinking about past experiences of their colleagues resulted in the development of both a to-do list and a list of don'ts for technology convergence. These lists covered everything from setting up a contract to appointing the team. Interestingly, when the CoP submitted their results to upper management, upper management felt the CoP had been too superficial in its investigations. Management encouraged the CoP to worry less about being intrusive and be more concerned with the impact the CoP would have on Beta-Telco as a whole. Essentially, Beta-Telco wanted the CoP to dig deeper, ask more questions, and get more payoff from the CoPs.

Conclusion

I hope you have found this book to an excellent introduction into Socratic questioning. I hope you can see yourself using these techniques at work and in your everyday life to help you reach your goals and reach success. From trying to define vague concepts that can have many different definitions to persuading your boss to see your point of view for why you deserve a raise, the Socratic method is a reliable technique you can count on.

Keep in mind some of the characteristics of the Socratic method, and it's sure to help you on your way as you become more comfortable applying the technique in your daily life. Remember that Socrates practiced his philosophy by using simple conversation. It can be harder to persuade someone in your direction if you're beating them over the head with facts and figures and judgments. Approach situations as if they were a conversation, and don't forget making assumptions can be helpful as long as you can justify your thinking.

Asking questions and searching for the "why" when you're at work can be something that sets you apart from your coworkers. I encourage you to reflect on your experiences and implement Socratic questioning techniques in the office. You may find yourself headed toward a leadership role if you aren't in one already. However, don't forget the value of Socratic questioning in the family. Children don't come with instruction manuals, and as a parent, you come across situations that you're not quite sure how to handle. If you can get to the root cause of your child's behavior, it can help you permanently resolve the issue versus implementing a temporary punishment that may be ineffective.

Thank you for taking the time to read this book and learn the principles presented. I hope you take the time to seek out opportunities to use Socratic questioning and then do so with confidence. Don't worry if you're a bit unsure at first. The more you practice, the more confident you will become. Just remember, this isn't an argument or a debate. All you need to do is have a conversation, just like Socrates.

Steven

References

1. https://plato.stanford.edu/entries/socrates/
2. https://www.britannica.com/biography/So crates
3. https://academyofideas.com/2013/04/the-ideas-of-socrates/
4. https://qz.com/1348203/a-neuroscientist-who-studies-rage-says-were-all-capable-of-doing-something-terrible/
5. https://www.vice.com/en_us/article/gqmz 4m/how-criminals-justify-crimes-psychology-gangsters-uk

6. https://www.prolificliving.com/the-greatest-discovery-of-all-getting-to-know-yourself/

7. https://www.youtube.com/watch?v=yIbV1nzOqgM&t=127s

8. https://www.thoughtco.com/what-was-the-charge-against-socrates-121060

9. https://www.quickanddirtytips.com/relationships/professional/how-to-persuade-effectively

10. https://www.danpink.com/2012/04/how-to-move-people-with-two-irrational-questions/

11. https://www.therapistaid.com/therapy-worksheet/socratic-questioning

12. https://www.researchgate.net/profile/Robert_Friedberg/publication/262141556_Guidelines_for_the_effective_use_of_Socratic_dialogue_in_cognitive_therapy/links/53f25a950cf2bc0c40e8780b/Guidelines-for-the-effective-use-of-Socratic-dialogue-in-cognitive-therapy.pdf

13. https://www.therapistaid.com/worksheets/socratic-questioning.pdf

14. https://hbswk.hbs.edu/archive/how-leaders-use-questions

15. https://www.google.com/url?sa=t&rct=j&q=&esrc=s&source=web&cd=11&cad=rja&uact=8&ved=2ahUKEwierMTPpu3lAhXOZd8KHTGKAA8QFjAKegQIABAC&url=http%3A%2F%2Fwww.ejkm.com%2Fissue%2Fdownload.html%3FidArticle%3D168&usg=AOvVaw3SriwDllTdlvrXVmc4YvSY